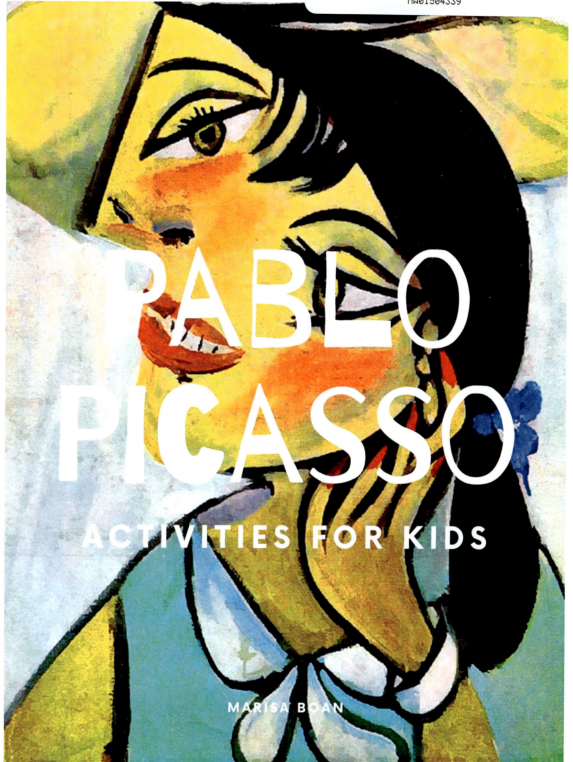

PABLO PICASSO

ACTIVITIES FOR KIDS

MARISA BOAN

Pablo Picasso

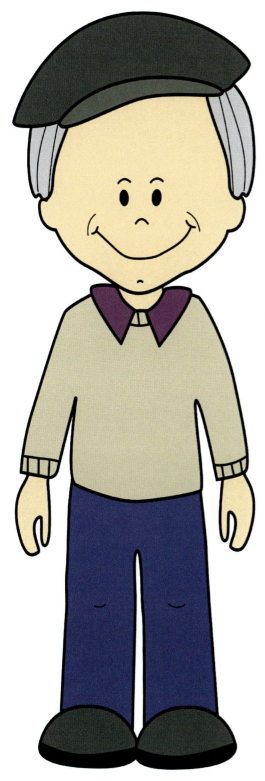

Pablo Picasso was born in Malaga, Spain on October 25, 1881. His father, Jose Ruiz y Blasco, was an artist and art professor who gave Pablo art lessons. Pablo liked to draw from an early age. According to his mother, his first word was "piz" when he was trying to say "lapiz," the Spanish word for pencil. Pablo liked to draw from an early age and his mother encouraged him to become an artist.

When he was fourteen years old Pablo attended a famous art school in Barcelona, A few years later he went to another school in Madrid. However, Pablo did not want to paint like everyone else in art school. He wanted to create something new in his own style. He preferred to spend his time visiting museums in Madrid like the famous Prado Museum.

Blue Period (1901-1904)
In 1901, Pablo's close friend died. Pablo was living in Paris, France at the time and became very sad. For the next few years most of his painting used a lot of blue paint and had sad figures in them. Some people say he painted in the color blue because he was "feeling blue" and was sad.

Rose Period (1904 - 1906)
Picasso began to feel better and was no longer so sad about losing his friend. He also fell in love . He began to use warmer colors in his paintings including pinks, reds, oranges, and beiges. This happier period in his life is called the Rose Period. During this period he painted happy scenes of people enjoying themselves.

Cubism (1907 - 1921)
In 1907 Picasso tried a new style of painting that he really liked. He started to paint his figures in shapes and broken up into pieces. By 1909 he had helped create a new style of painting called Cubism. In Cubism the pieces of a painting are broken up into shapes, like a puzzle. The pieces are put back together again in a different way. Sometimes the figures are easy to recognize. Sometimes they look funny. Sometimes they are like a puzzle you have to figure out.

Pablo Picasso is considered the greatest artist of the 20th century. He took risks and developed his own style. He followed his dream of becoming a painter. He created a new style of painting that many other painters followed. He changed his style depending on his feelings and became a great famous artist.

CHARACTER TRAITS

able
active
adventurous
ambitious
blue
bold
brainy
brave
bright
brilliant
charming
cheerful
clever
clumsy
confident
considerate
courageous
cowardly
curious
daring
determined
dull
dutiful
eager
energetic
excited
expert
fair
faithful
fearless
foolish
fortunate

friendly
funny
gentle
giving
good
happy
Harsh
helpful
honest
hopeful
hopeless
humorous
independent
intelligent
jealous
kindly
lazy
leader
lively
lonely
loving
loyal
lucky
mature
mean
messy
nice
noisy
old
picky
pleasant
polite

poor
popular
positive
proud
quiet
responsible
restless
rich
rough
rude
sad
safe
scared
serious
sharp
short
shy
silly
skillful
sly
smart
spoiled
strict
stubborn
sweet
talented
tall
thankful
trustworthy
warm
wise
young

Character Traits

Use adjectives to describe this artist.
Write the adjectives on the boxes next to the artist.

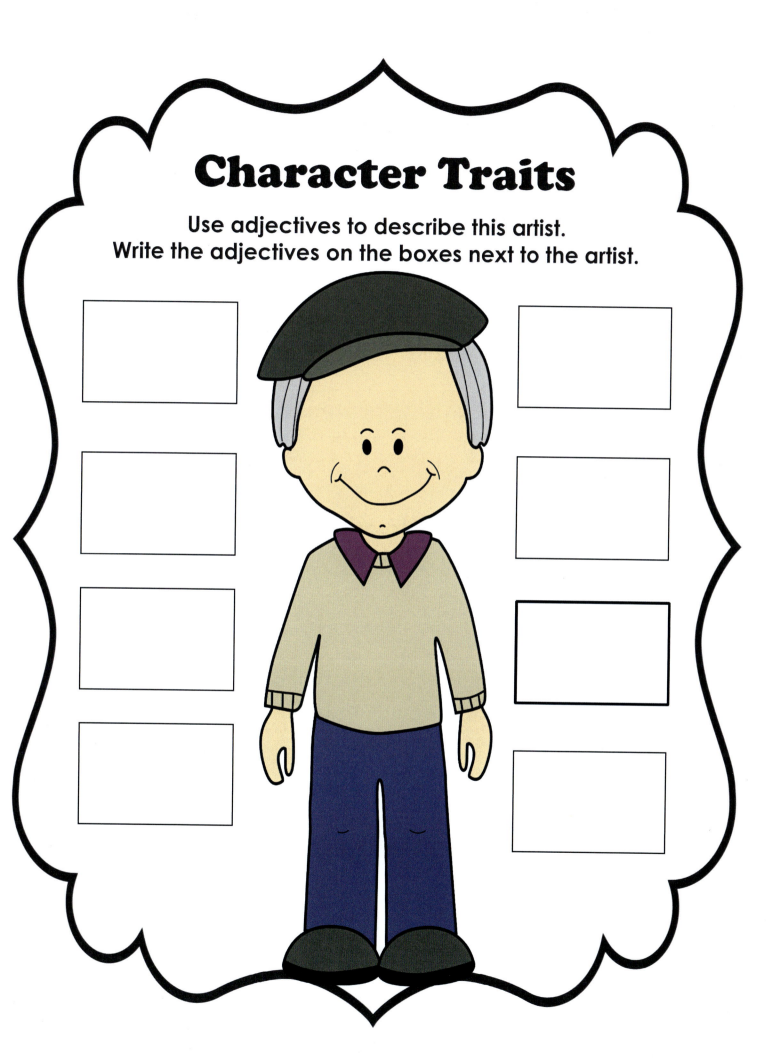

Sequence of Events

Number the following events in order from 1-6 or cut them cut and paste them in order in your notebook.

	Pablo's close friend died. Pablo was living in Paris, France at the time and became very sad.

	Picasso began to feel better and was no longer so sad about losing his friend. He also fell in love

	Pablo Picasso was born in Spain on October 25, 1881

	He changed his style depending on his feelings and became a great famous artist.

	By 1909 he had helped create a new style of painting called Cubism.

	He began to use warmer colors in his paintings including pinks, reds, oranges, and beiges.

VOCABULARY MATCHING

Draw a line from the word to the definition

• artist

• Blue Period

• Cubism

• painting

• Rose Period

• A sad time when Picasso painted in blue

• a style of painting with shapes like a puzzle

• art created with brushes and paint

• A happy time in Picasso's life

• a creative person who draws or paints

MISSING LETTERS

P _ r _ s   _____

ar _ ist   _____

_ ol _ r   _____

mu _ _ um   _____

cu _ ism   _____

r _ _ e   _____

S _ _ in   _____

_ ai _ tin _ _____

_ ale _ t   _____

_ lue   _____

MAKING WORDS

Use the letters below to make some new words!

2 letter words	3 letter words	4 letter words	5 letter words	6 letter words	Seven or more letter words

S O S S A C I P O B A P

The Stories They Tell

Look at the painting
and write a story about it

Word Search

```
p  a  r  i  s  b  l  u  e
i  p  e  r  i  o  d  c  j
c  t  m  c  s  a  q  c  t
a  f  k  o  g  l  j  l  p
s  d  i  l  a  o  s  r  v
s  g  u  o  b  p  h  i  c
o  t  a  r  t  i  s  t  u
g  r  f  a  m  o  u  s  b
m  r  o  s  e  b  l  o  i
d  e  f  d  c  u  c  y  s
k  m  u  s  e  u  m  n  m
```

period   Picasso
color   museum
blue   rose
Paris   cubism
artist   famous

ILLUSTRATED ACROSTIC POEM

Write an Acrostic Poem
about this Artist
and draw a picture in
the box

C _____

U _____

B _____

i _____

S _____

M _____

LOOKiNG AT ART

List 3 things you see in this painting.

Portrait of Olga

Draw your favorite part of the painting in this circle

What is the setting of this painting?

List all of the colors you can see in this painting.

Take A Second Look

Describe the painting
in your own words

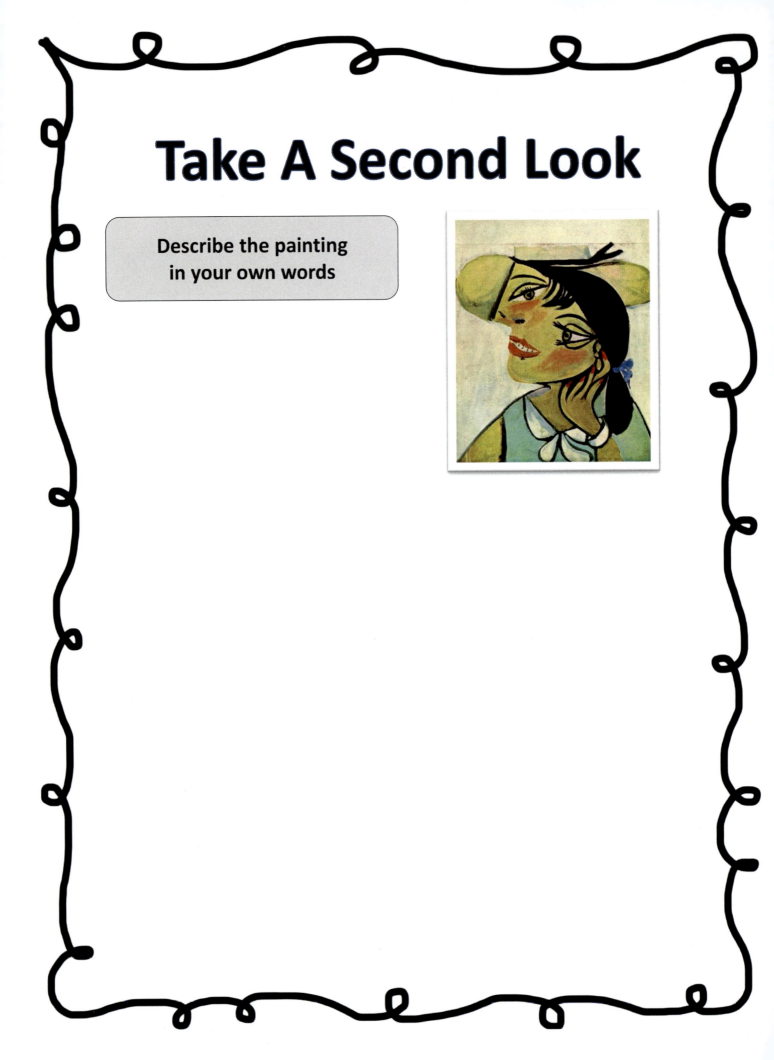

Role Model

**Make a List of All the Things
You Like About This Person**

PAINTING MATCH UP

Write the name of each painting in the box below it

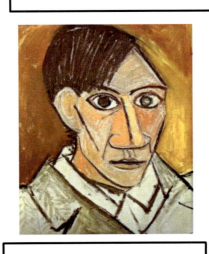

Self Portrait	Three Musicians	Child with a Dove
Woman Sitting in an Armchair	Bathers	The Old Guitarist

Story Elements

Look at the painting and identify the story elements

Setting

When and where does
it take place?

Characters

Who is in the painting?
Who do you think they are?

Theme

What is the big idea? What is
the central message of this
painting?

Plot

What is happening?

Design Your Own Picasso

Famous Quotes

The world doesn't make sense, so why should I paint pictures that do.

I paint objects as I think them, not as I see them.

Everything you can imagine is real.

I do not seek. I find

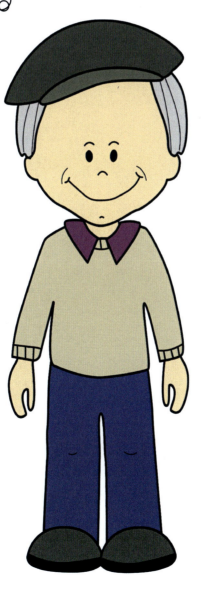

Which is your favorite quote?

Pick one to write about in your notebook.

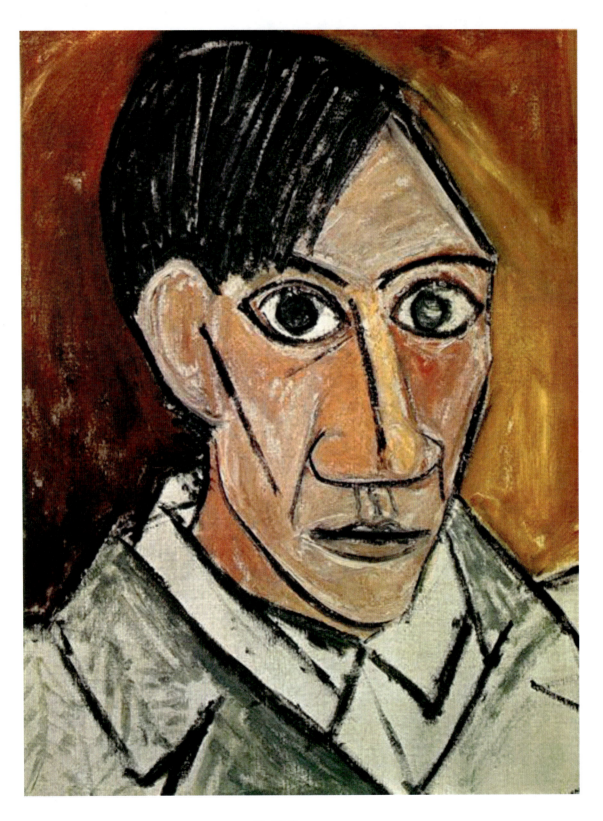

Self Portrait

Portrait of Olga

Compare & Contrast

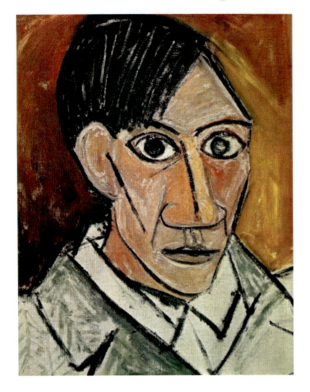

Self Portrait

Portrait of Olga

ALIKE

DIFFERENT

ARTBOP

What shapes and colors did the artist use in this painting?

Do you like or dislike this painting? Why or why not?

Portrait of Olga
by Pablo Picasso

What are 5 things you see in this painting?

Draw your own version of this painting.

What is one question you would like to ask the artist about this painting?

Portrait de femme au col d'hermine (Olga)
Portrait of a woman with an ermine collar (Olga)

Portrait of Olga

MEET THE ARTIST SERIES

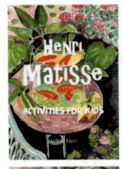

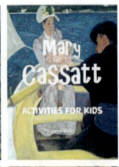
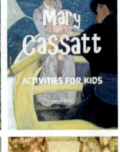

Each Activity Book has over 20 pages of **Reading & Writing Activities**

LEARN - COLOR - CREATE

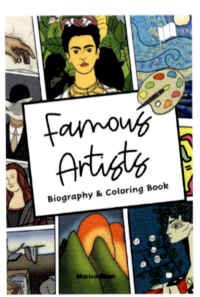
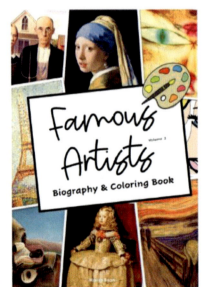
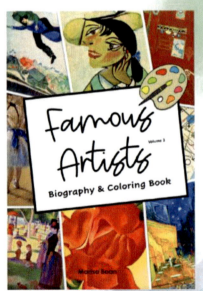

CHOOSE FROM THREE DIFFERENT VOLUMES!

MAGICSPELLSFORTEACHERS.COM

MISSING LETTERS KEY

P _ r _ s   _____Paris__

ar _ ist   ___artist_____

_ ol _ r   color_____

mu _ _ um   ___museum___

cu _ ism   _cubism_____

R _ _ e   _Rose_____

S _ _ in   __Spain____

_ ai _ t in _ _painting____

_ ale _ t   __talent__

_ lue   Blue_____

Word Search

p	a	r	i	s	i	s	b	l	u	e
i	p	e	r	i	o	d	c	j
c	t	m	c	s	a	q	c	t
a	f	k	o	g	l	j	l	p
s	d	i	l	a	o	s	r	v
s	g	u	o	b	p	h	i	c
o	t	a	r	t	i	s	t	u
g	r	f	a	m	o	u	s	b
m	r	o	s	e	b	l	o	i
d	e	f	d	c	u	c	y	s
k	m	u	s	e	u	m	n	m

period   Picasso
color   museum
blue   rose
Paris   cubism
artist   famous

PAINTING MATCH UP

Write the name of each painting in the box below it

Woman Sitting in an Armchair

The Old Guitarist

Three Musicians

Bathers

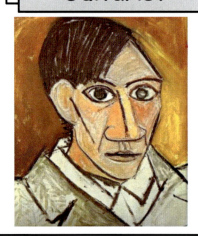

Self Portrait

Child with a Dove

MAGICSPELLSFORTEACHERS.COM

Available at

amazon

Made in the USA
Middletown, DE
25 May 2025

76041856R00018